Small Pets

Hamsters

by Chris Henwood

W. Foulsham & Co. Ltd.
London · New York · Toronto · Cape Town · Sydney

To my wonderful wife Janet who has had to put up with more hamsters than we dare to count.

Acknowledgements

During the time that I have kept hamsters I have had both my knowledge and stock increased by a number of people namely: Roy Robinson, Hazel Williams, Mike and Wendy Stokes-Claire, Denis Holmes and Ron Willis. To these and others I extend my grateful thanks.

Photographs Mike O'Neill

W. Foulsham & Company Limited
Yeovil Road, Slough, Berkshire, SL1 4JH

ISBN 0-572-01348-5

Photoset in Great Britain by Filmtype Services Limited, Scarborough, North Yorkshire and printed in Spain by Cayfosa. Barcelona.
Dep. Leg. B-33251-1985

Contents

1 The Golden Hamster

There are at least 54 different species or sub-species of hamster distributed throughout the world, but by far the best known is the Golden hamster. The Golden hamster is one of the most popular of all small pets. It is unique in that its origins in the pet market are very well chronicled, although very little is actually known about it in the wild.

Russian Hamsters, Satin coated and normal variety

The first recorded discovery of the Golden or Syrian hamster (*Mesocricetus auratus* as it is known to science) was in 1839 when Mr G. R. Waterhouse presented the Zoological Society of London with a skull and skin of a female hamster on his return from Syria. The first live animals known to have been kept in Britain were owned by James Skene who, on retiring from his post of British Consul to Syria in 1880, brought a colony of hamsters back to Britain. This colony survived until about 1910 when the last individuals died.

It was not until April 1930 that the species was again brought to the attention of science. Professor Israel Aharoni, while on a scientific expedition near Mount Aleppo in Syria, dug out a female and her litter of young. Eight of the young were taken to the Hebrew University at Jerusalem and there placed under the care of Dr Ben-Manahem. Of these eight, four escaped, one female was killed by the male, who in turn mated with the two remaining females. By the end of the first year in captivity this trio had produced a total of 364 young.

Until 1971 when another group of these hamsters was found, this trio was responsible for all the Golden hamsters in captivity throughout the world.

Breeding stock was dispatched to several countries, arriving in Britain in 1933 when Dr S. Adler of the Microbiological Institute in Jerusalem presented two pairs to Mr E. Windle, a fellow at the National Institute for Medical Research in London. For a number of years they were bred only in laboratories and at the

London Zoo. Because of the Second World War it was not until 1945 that individuals arrived onto the pet market in Great Britain, but from then on the Golden hamster has never lost its popularity.

It may have been the scientists that first noticed that hamsters made good pets, but it was the mothers that made hamsters the successful and popular pets they are today. They often dislike the pet mouse because of its skinny tail and the fact that it can have a rather unpleasant smell. Hamsters on the other hand have neither of these. They are very friendly, inquisitive animals, and extremely clean in their habits. They even have a corner of the cage that they use as a toilet. They are not too small, measuring about 17 cm (7 ins) in length.

Hamsters must be housed on their own as their natural habit is to fight other hamsters they meet, unless it is to mate, and even then breeding females are often aggressive to the males and in the wild each sex has its own separate burrow. It is therefore quite the reverse of cruel to keep a hamster on its own, in fact the golden rule is always one hamster, one cage.

Hamsters are naturally nocturnal, sleeping for most of the day and becoming active at dusk. In captivity they usually become more active during the day, particularly when kept in a busy room. They have a life span of about three years, although they have been known to reach seven on very rare occasions.

2 Housing

Before you buy a hamster, it is a good idea to have the cage ready, so that when you bring your new pet home you can place it straight into its cage and allow it to get used to its new surroundings.

There are many types of cages designed especially for hamsters, which can be obtained from most pet shops. Some are very elaborate and expensive, but others can be bought at reasonable prices. All types of materials are used for these cages including perspex, plastic, metal and glass. Plastic is perhaps the best material of all, being both warm and easy to keep

Golden Dominant Spot Short-haired female on typical pet hamster cage

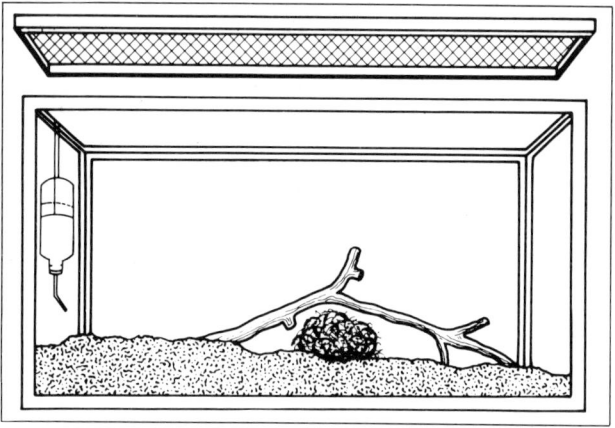

Tank converted for hamster

clean. Metal on the other hand is cold and is liable to go rusty after prolonged use. Wood is not suitable as, being rodents, hamsters are likely to gnaw and chew their way through wood and escape in a very short time.

Probably the cheapest and cleanest way to retain a single hamster is to convert an old fish tank. This can be done by replacing the fish tank top, normally supplied to hold the lights, with a wooden-framed wire mesh top. The mesh used should be 1.5 cm (½ inch) squared, young animals are likely to be able to squeeze through any larger than this. Do not use chicken wire; it may well be cheaper than the square mesh but it is very soft and can easily be chewed through.

One of the most recent types of cage to arrive on the market is the multi-unit system that can be added to again and again. On the whole I have found that although these are very attractive cages, even when they are made up of a great number of parts they are still too small. This is particularly true of the up and down pipes that connect the various parts and levels. The diameter of these pipes is only suitable for young animals and not for adults, particularly those that are of show standard.

Whatever cage you finally choose it should offer forward vision and some climbing facilities, even if these are only the wire sides of the cage itself. The bottom of the cage should be covered with approximately 5 cm (2 ins) of fresh, coarse sawdust or wood shavings. Never use cat litter, fine sawdust or sand as this will be inhaled when the hamster is digging or nosing about in the cage and will lead to both nasal and eye troubles. Provide plenty of nesting materials. The best of these is always good quality meadow hay, but alternative materials that can be used are vegetable parchment or soft toilet or kitchen tissue. Never use cotton wool or the cotton waste materials often sold in pet shops; these are likely to cause a bloated stomach if swallowed, and may even cause death. Straw should also not be used as it is much too sharp, and again is likely to cause eye troubles. A nest box is not really neccessary as hamsters tend to make their own nests and adapt the amount of materials used according to the external temperature of the cage.

A useful addition to any hamster cage is a piece of wood. Wood from fruit trees is the best, but any other non-coniferous tree can be used. This wood provides both something for your hamster to climb on and something to chew at.

Exercise wheels can be given to hamsters, but they should not be left in the cage all the time as the animal is then likely to overstrain itself by using the wheel too often. They can in fact be so habit-forming that I have known females to allow their litter to die as they are more interested in the wheel than looking after their young. I have also known animals actually to run themselves to death through exhaustion. Three or four hours exercise on the wheel each night is more than enough. Exercise wheels should never be given to females that are either pregnant or that have litters in the nest, nor to long haired males, as they are likely to get their long coat caught in the wheel.

The cage itself should be positioned in an airy well-lit area, out of direct sunlight and away from draughts, where there is an even temperature of 16-22°C (64-72°F).

3 Varieties of Golden Hamster

The original colouring of the wild hamster is the familiar golden-brown, and for some fifteen years after its capture this was the only known colour. However, nature occasionally creates variations in the forms of mutations, and when more than one of these mutations occur, these can be combined by selective breeding to make yet another. Over the years, the Golden hamster has produced more than its fair share of mutations. These have been selectively bred by various breeders to enhance and preserve them so that others may appreciate them too.

There is therefore a wide variety of colours of hamsters for you to choose from and before going into colour breeding, or even deciding exactly what colours to keep, you must ensure that you know exactly why the various colours occur and what they look like.

Dominant and Recessive Inheritance

There are two forms of inheritance, recessive and dominant, the recessive being the most common form. A colour is known to be recessive when it disappears in crosses with the original wild colour, gold. For example, when a Black-Eyed Cream variety is mated to a Golden, the youngsters which result are all golden in colour, similar to the golden parent. This proves that golden is dominant to cream and vice versa – the cream is recessive to the golden. If mated together, the youngsters will give birth to 75 per cent golden young and 25 per cent cream young. However, if you mate them back to the cream parent, they will give birth to 50 per cent golden young and 50 per cent cream young.

This shows what is known as the typical 3:1 ratio, which plays an important part in genetics. The fact that the cream colour does not reappear until the second generation need not worry the breeder because once it has recurred the cream youngsters are true breeding and will not revert to golden if mated together.

The first cross of any two colours is known as the F_1 generation and when these are mated together, they produce the F_2 generation.

A dominant form of inheritance is when a colour does not disappear in crosses with the normal golden. For example, a Golden mated to a Golden White Spot will produce Golden White Spot young in the first litter. This proves that the white spot is a dominant inheritance. If two of these young are mated together, the youngsters will be 75 per cent white spot and 25 per cent normal golden. If you mate the F_1 youngsters to a normal Golden, the resulting litter would be of 50 per cent Golden White Spot and 50 per cent Golden.

Split Inheritance

One point to remember is that whether you are

dealing with a dominant or a recessive inheritance, a colour is not neccessarily lost if it
does not appear in the young. A hamster which
is golden, cream, white or cinnamon, is more
than likely to be 'split'. This means that it carries
one or more colours. For example, if a Golden
was mated to a Cream, the young should be
Golden as this is dominant. If, in fact, the litter
included three Goldens and one Cream, then
you know that the Golden is 'split for', or 'a
carrier of' Cream.

The split animal can be recognised in a number of ways. If a hamster produces more than
one colour among its offspring then it is certainly a split animal. When two colour varieties
are mated together it is almost certain that the
youngsters will be split animals of one type or
another, and the offspring will be split for the
colour that has disappeared. For example, if a
Golden is mated to a Cream, the young will
appear golden, but they are, in fact, split for
cream.

Standards

Today there are many different varieties of
Golden hamster available – some are new,
some old, some popular and some not so. Each
variety, however, has what is known as a standard. This is really a description of the particular variety – what an ideal animal of that
particular variety should look like. I have listed
here a number of standards of various varieties
both common and rare, popular and un-
popular. They give a general idea of what to

look for in both exhibition or show animals and also in breeding stock.

They are not, however, always exactly the same as the judging standards listed by the various hamsters clubs, for a number of reasons. Some of the more popular colours available on the pet market are not recognised by the hamster clubs. The Red Eyed Cream, and others, although recognised by the clubs, are judged to an impossible standard. Members are attempting to have the standards changed.

The best way of seeing exactly what a particular standard or variety should look like is to visit a breeder of exhibition or show animals, or better still to visit an actual show where you are likely to see more examples than any one breeder can show you. However, I hope that the following list will give you at least an idea of what to look for.

Normal Golden

The overall colour of the normal Golden should be a deep brown that is uniform over the head, back and sides. The under colour may vary slightly from a deep slate blue to a medium shade of grey. The belly fur is an off white verging on a dirty cream. The crescents and throat will also show the same colour as the belly which gives the normal Golden a confused demarcation line between these and the black cheek flashes. It is difficult to establish the exact ear colour, but ideally they should be as dark grey as possible – almost black. The eye colour should be jet black.

Dark Golden

This is one of my personal favourite varieties. The body colour is a deep, rich mahogany red that is over-ticked with black guard hairs. The black ticking should be more pronounced over the head and back and in well-marked animals there is a definite circle of black shading around the eyes. The under colour is a very dark slate grey over the whole of the body. The belly fur and throat are a pale pearly grey. The crescents are white and there is a strong contrast between these and the jet black cheek flashes. The ears should be as dark grey as possible – nearly black, and the eyes black.

Dark Golden Short-haired male (note hip spots)

Black Eyed Cream

There is rather a lot of argument over the exact

shade of colour that this variety should be, ranging as it does from a pale off white to a rich deep apricot shade. Ideally it should, in my opinion, be a warm creamy peach colour with a slight tinge of pink. It is a self coloured animal and should have no other colour on the body. Most Black Eyed Creams do however have a small white chin stripe, running from the lower jaw to the chest, and although this is frowned upon it is rare that you will find a Black Eyed Cream without any white on its chin.

Black Eyed Cream Long-haired Satin male

Red Eyed Cream

This colour variety is becoming increasingly popular and is providing a rival to the Black Eyed Cream because the cream of this variety is a much more stable shade. The ears are pale grey or flesh coloured.

Ruby Eyed Cream

A beautiful variety of cream but unfortunately rather rare. The males of this variety are sterile as adults, and the females have to be out crossed to split males to retain the line. The whole body should be a pale shade of cream with no tendency to the apricot shade of the Black Eyed Cream. It has a very noticeable pinkish tinge. The ears are pale grey to flesh coloured.

Dark Eared Albino

The Dark Eared Albino is obviously an incomplete albino because of its coloured ears. It is thought that this variety is equivalent to the Himalayan varieties in other small rodents. The entire body should be pure white to the roots with no foreign markings whatever. In young hamsters of this variety the ears begin to darken at about three months of age. Until this time they are flesh coloured, and by the time the hamster is fully mature the transition to full coloured grey ears is complete. The eyes of the Dark Eared Albino are a deep pink, which darkens with age until they take on the appearance of ruby. Because this colour is of the albino family it is recessive to all other colours except that of the Flesh Eared Albino. Other colours can be split for Dark Eared Albino, but it cannot be split for any other colour.

Flesh Eared Albino

The coat colour is again white to the roots with no tendency to yellow. The ears are flesh coloured.

Flesh Eared Albino Short-haired female

Dark Grey Short-haired male

Dark Grey

This again is a colour that is becoming more and more popular. The whole of the back, sides and head should be a definite, dark grey, with a slate blue under colour. The belly fur and crescents are pale grey. The cheek flashes are black. The ears are also dark grey and should match the body colour as nearly as possible. The eyes are jet black.

Black

This variety is not a true Black as in the Gerbil or Cavy but a 'false' black, produced by combining the Black Eyed Cream and the umborous or sooty gene, although recently the colour has been greatly improved by the introduction of the Dark Grey. It is a self coloured animal. However many of the individuals being bred have a small white chin stripe as in the Black Eyed Cream and there is argument as to whether this should be allowed or not. Should a true Black mutation occur in the future then it is likely that this variety will fall from the popularity it has gained over the past few years. Its name is also likely to be changed to the more genetically correct Sable. The entire coat colour should ideally be black, as solid and even as is possible and carried well down into the fur, although a light circle around each eye is permissible. The ear and eye colour is black.

Chocolate

A variety produced by combining the Black

Black Long-haired female

Chocolate Short-haired female

with Rust, another self coloured animal with the same white chin stripe problem as the Black. At the moment the colour is similar to that of milk chocolate but it is darkening with selective breeding. The ears are flesh coloured and the eyes black.

Sooty Varieties

Other varieties that are produced by combining the umborous or 'sooty gene' with others are the various so called sooty varieties. These are basically normal coloured animals such as the Golden, Cinnamon, Grey and soon, with a heavy ticking of black.

Cinnamon

Probably the most striking of all of the hamster colour varieties, the body of the cinnamon should be a bright clear orange with a bluish grey undercolour. The intensive orange should be the aim of breeders of this variety, pale animals should be rejected from the breeding programme. The belly is a creamy white rather than pure white. The crescents should also be white whereas the cheek flashes are a rich cinnamon brown and clearly distinct. The ears are a cinnamon brown, the eyes a deep claret red.

Rust

A very similar colour to the Cinnamon although tending to a slightly more brownish with a less well defined under colour. The eyes are black rather than red.

Cinnamon Umborous (Sooty) Satin Short-haired male

Tortoiseshell

The Tortoiseshell is a sex-linked bi-coloured animal, and although it is rather attractive on its own it is usually combined with white, either by the introduction of the White Spotted or Banded gene. The markings are large blotches of colour consisting of a balanced pattern of coloured, yellow and white patches. These patches should be clear and distinct with a minimum of brindling. The white areas should not predominate over the coloured and yellow patches. The coloured area can be of any solid variety, for example: Cinnamon, Golden, Grey or Cream. The yellow should as near as possible conform to the standard yellow variety. The ears and the eyes should conform to the full coloured varieties.

Tortoiseshell and White Short-haired female

Banded

This is another very popular variety. It can be of any colour – Golden, Cream, Cinnamon, Rust, Yellow and so on. It gets its name from a wide band of white that encircles its middle. The standard usually calls for the band to be approximately one third of the width of the body. The demarcation line between the white and coloured area should be crisp and well defined. The colour of both the eyes and ears should be as for that of the full coloured variety.

Golden Banded Satin Short-haired male

Dominant Spot and Piebald

These are two separate varieties but are very similar in appearance and it is often very difficult to tell them apart at a glance. The former is, however, a dominant variety while the latter

Golden Dominant Spot Short-haired female

is a reccessive. Both can be combined with any of the solid colours and even with Banded. The actual spotting varies a great deal from individual to individual, but in general the animal should have the appearance of a white animal with coloured markings. The markings should be sharply defined, evenly broken into approximately equal amounts of coloured and white over the entire coat. Both the eyes and ears should conform to the solid varieties.

Yellow

The Yellow is another of my particular favourites. It is a colour that has caused some very heated arguments over the years in the hamster world. It is now generally agreed that the top colour should be a rich yellow, with even black ticking overall, the top colour being carried well down into the fur with a uniform ivory under colour at the base of the hairs. The belly fur should be the same ivory colour. The cheek flashes should be finely ticked and the crescents ivory. The ears are dark grey and the eyes black. Yellow is the variety that when combined with Golden will produce Tortoiseshell.

Yellow Short-haired male with full cheek pouches

Lilac

One of the newest colour varieties and one that is gaining popularity. It is really a combination of the Cinnamon and Dark Grey varieties. The colour is a soft pale grey with a slightly pinkish tone with a slightly darker undercoat and free from any shading. The belly is similar but slightly lighter in colour, as are the chest bands. The crescents are white. The eyes are claret red and the ears pale grey brown.

Lilac Short-haired male

Other Varieties

These are just a few of the colour varieties. Among others that occur are Roan, Caramel, Mink, Copper, Beige, Stone, Light Grey and Ivory. All of these can be combined with the following coat or fur type varieties.

Satin

The Satin was the first of the changes of fur type to appear. Satinisation increases the attractiveness of any colour, it makes the coat shine as though it were highly polished. A Satin should not be mated to a Satin, but to a normal coated animal, as two Satins mated together will produce animals of a double satin coat, the hair of which is very sparse. The Satin can be of any accepted colour or markings and can also

Rex

It is a rather sad fact that this variety has been greatly neglected by many experienced breeders. The reason for this is not clear, for I find that it is a very impressive variety if bred correctly. In fact I worked for almost three years on this one variety to obtain a recognised stan- be combined with the Rex and Long-haired varieties.

Umborous Golden (Sooty) Short-haired Rex female

dard for it. The Rex coat comes about because the guard hairs of the normal coat are very much shortened. This has the effect that the coat will not lie flat as normal but stands up in a velvet-like finish. The Rex can be bred in any of the coat colours and also combined with the Satin and the Long-haired. However, I have found that the best combinations are the Creams, Whites and Chocolate. The reason for this is that these varieties have no under colour to show through the top coat. I also do not like Rex combined with the Long-haired variety. It is acceptable in the female, but in the males the combination is a mess. The coat should be very dense and soft to the touch. The whiskers of the Rex are short and very curly.

Long-haired

In the United States of America this variety is often known as the Angora. It was first discovered in that country in the early 1970s and arrived in Britain a few years later. It was a great curiosity at the time and has since attracted a lot of admiration and a very strong following. It is interesting to note that the long flowing coat is only present in the males, the coat of the female being quite a bit shorter. The Long-haired can be combined with Satin and Rex and bred in any of the colour varieties, but it looks much better in the self coloured animals than those that are patterned or marked. In the Golden and similar colours, for example, the cheek flashes and crescents are lost, giving the animal a washed out appearance.

Black Long-haired Rex male and Red Eyed Cream Long-haired Rex male

4 Choosing Your Hamster

When buying a hamster, or for that matter any other small pet, it is always wise to go to a good pet shop or private breeder. If you intend to breed or show your stock, it is almost essential to go to a private breeder. Please do not try to look around for bargains or the cheapest animals – good hamsters are not expensive.

The best age hamster to buy is between seven and twelve weeks of age. Baby hamsters are shy and easily frightened so it is useless to attempt to tame a baby too early.

Pet shops on the whole vary in the way they keep and display hamsters. Keeping them in individual cages is best, but some shops do not always have the room to do this, and keep their young animals together in a collective cage. In this case, unless the animals are under eight weeks of age, it is better not to choose a female from a cage that contains animals of both sexes. You are very likely to end up with a pregnant female and a lot more hamsters than you intended.

Take your time, ask the shop assistant or breeder to show you as many animals as you wish to see. You may be asked whether you would like a male or a female, but sex is not too important if you are only going to keep one animal.

Do not choose a hamster just by observing it in its cage. Have the owner take it out of the cage and place it on a counter or table where you can have a closer look at it. After the hamster has been put down, do not try to pick it up at once. Give it a chance to become acquainted with you, perhaps by offering it a titbit. Once it seems to be happy, extend your hand slowly and stroke it. Remember it will still be rather nervous, so do not make any sudden moves.

If the hamster does not scurry away from your hand, let it hover for a moment so that it sees the hand, then close your hand gently but firmly around its entire body so that it is cradled in your closed fist. Never reach quickly down from above to pick up your hamster, as in the wild this is how it would be attacked by its enemies and you are almost sure to be nipped. Instead cup you hands around it and scoop it up into your open hands, placing your thumbs over the animal's back as you do so, as this will prevent it from jumping into the air.

When you have picked it up successfully, inspect it for sores or large wounds; if it has any then refuse it. Some scars may occur, particularly if the animals have been kept together a little too long, but this should not cause you to reject an animal if it is still friendly and the wounds are not large or infected.

5 Handling and Taming

Hamsters are short-sighted animals and therefore learn to know their owners mainly by smell and sound. An important part of getting your pet to know you is to speak to it at feeding times and any other time that it is up and about.

The best time of the day to start handling and taming your hamster is in the early evening when you feed it. Having placed the day's supply of food into the cage, a gentle tapping on the side of the cage will wake the hamster up. On no account poke your finger into the nest to wake it up, as this will startle it and it will then be likely to bite. When the hamster comes out and begins to pouch the food you can very gently stroke it, repeating this a few times so that it can get used to both the touch and smell of your hand. At first it may flinch or even run away, but this should not deter you; it will soon get used to you and sit quite still while you stroke it.

Do not at this point attempt to pick it up or grab at it. A little patience here will be well rewarded. Continue to stroke the hamster when it comes out for food for the next three or four nights then offer a titbit such as a piece of carrot, apple or sweet dry biscuit so that it will get used to receiving special food from your fingers.

Then obtain a small piece of stiff wire mesh and coax your hamster onto it. Once on the mesh, stroke it gently, talking to it, and then return it to the cage with a titbit. Again, repeat this for several nights, gradually closing your hand over the hamster. Within a few days you should be able to lift it off the wire and put it back into its cage. The object of this is to give the animal confidence in you and make it feel that your hand is a safe place for it to be in.

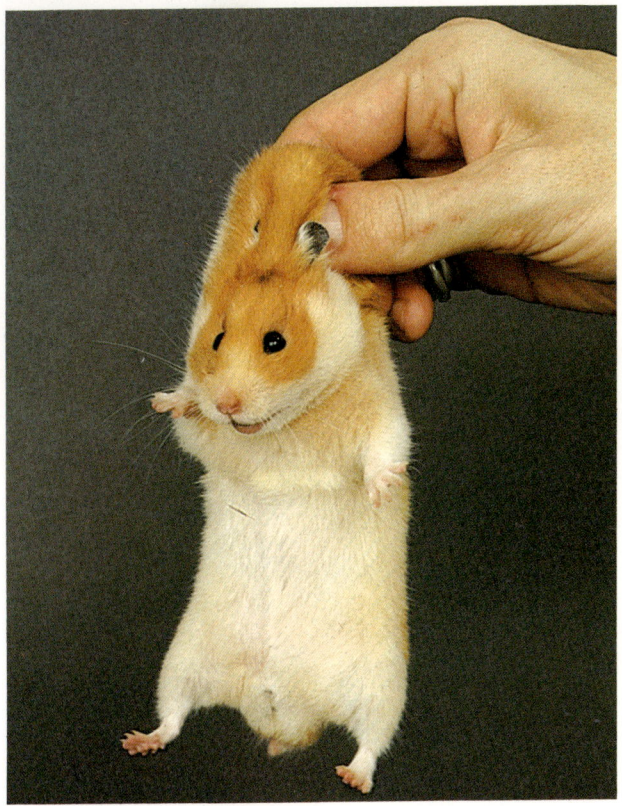

How to hold an untamed hamster

When stroking or picking up a hamster be sure to hold your hand so that the fingers are pointing towards the animal's rear, then let the hand curl gently underneath the hamster and lift it firmly. The reason for keeping your fingers towards the rear is to avoid being nipped by the hamster. Later on, when it has got used to you, it should not be necessary to do this. Do not attempt to pick up a young untamed animal in

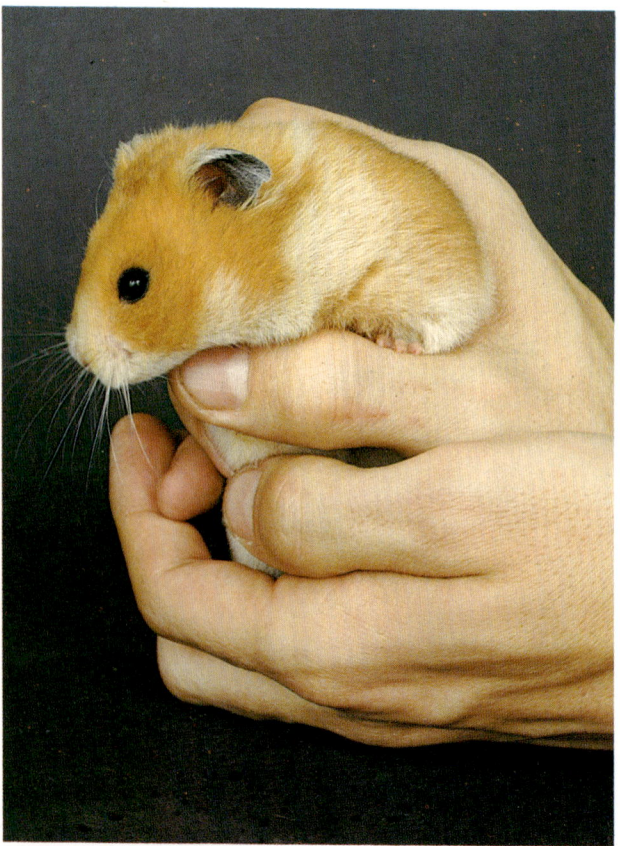

How to hold a tamed pet hamster

only one hand, as the sudden movement may well cause it to panic and it will try to jump or wriggle out of your grasp.

When lifting or carrying your animal any distance it is advisable to use cupped hands to avoid accidental falls. Remember, with hamsters gentle handling, speaking quietly and giving the occasional titbit is the quickest way to help it get to know you. If it is difficult to handle at first or even bites, it is probably because it is frightened and not because it is vicious.

Escapes and Recaptures

The average hamster spends a great deal of its time plotting and trying to work out a way to escape. It gnaws, digs, climbs, scratches and pushes for hours on end, and it is more than likely that one day it will actually manage to get out. This is not usually any cause for alarm, as unless the room is full of holes to the outside or under the floor, your hamster won't be far away, and you can usually catch it quite easily. In fact you may only realise that it is out when you catch sight of a little furry creature on top of the curtains or scurrying across the floor.

To catch your hamster all you need is a carrot, a bucket or a smooth metal waste bin and a few thick books or bricks. Place the bucket on the floor with the hamster cage open nearby. In the bottom of the bucket place some sawdust and bedding plus a small amount of food. Pile the books or bricks beside the bucket so that they form a sort of step ladder to the top of the bucket. Rub the carrot gently up the steps and then drop it into the bucket and leave it overnight. In the morning your escapee will be found sound asleep in the bottom of the bucket. It is very rare that this method fails.

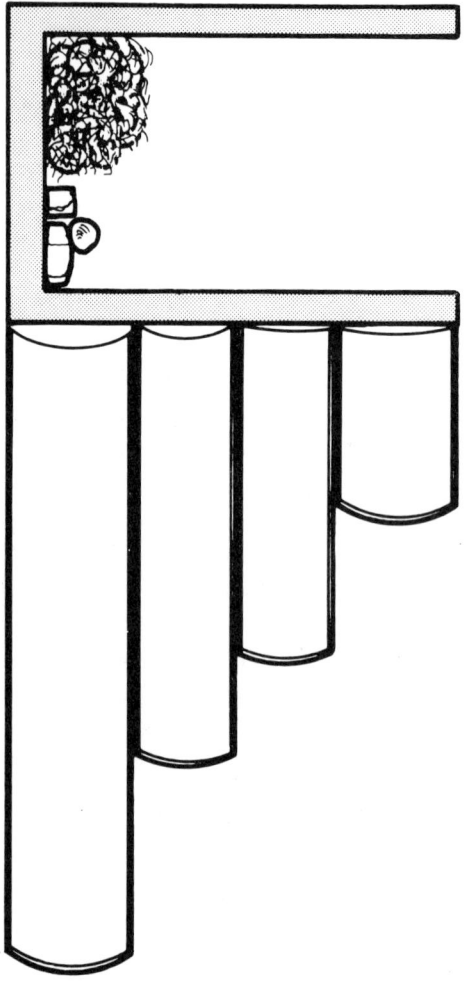

6 **Feeding Your Hamster**

Feeding your hamster is very simple as they will eat almost anything you care to give them. This does not mean that their food should consist of any old rubbish, but that it is up to you to make sure that their food is always of the highest quality, as the hamster is not very selective.

Hamsters are gnawing creatures and are therefore rather slow eaters. Their main diet consists of nuts, seeds and other hard foods, and although they are fond of some soft foods their major diet is of hard materials, which are chewed and digested slowly.

This helps to explain why they hoard so much of their food. In the wild, it is much less hazardous to take their time eating in their burrow rather than in an exposed spot. As with most rodents – and indeed humans – the best motto on food is that variety is the spice of life and the hamster certainly agrees with this.

Ready-mixed packeted hamster food is often available in the pet shops and in supermarkets, but I have found that these packs often contain poor quality food. By far the best, in my opinion, is the loose seed sold by most good pet shops and mixed especially for hamsters.

The basic diet of the hamster should ideally contain the following foods.

Cereals

Oats often form the basis of the diet. They can be purchased in two forms, whole and crushed. Although there is a larger amount of waste with crushed oats, I advise using this rather than whole oats as the husks are less sharp and if pouched are not likely to damage the lining of the cheek pouches.

Along with oats, wheat can be used as a basic food, often in equal parts. Wheat is very rich in vitamin E and is said greatly to assist fertility. Be careful not to give too much wheat, however, as it will become unpalatable and will be wasted.

Maize, or corn as it is sometimes known, can be obtained in either the cut, nibbled or flaked forms. All are useful in the hamster's diet, but do not give too much as this grain is a heating food. A great advantage of all forms of maize is that the hamster eats the whole seed and there is therefore no waste.

Pellets, Nuts and Seeds

Pellets are more commonly sold in the pet shops as rabbit pellets, but many other forms are available. They are a compound food and contain a balanced amount of food and vitamins. The pellets are a useful part of the diet but they should not be regarded as a complete diet on their own.

Sunflower seeds are one of the hamster's most relished food. They are rich in vitamin E and vegetable oil. Again, beware of excess, however, as this will cause both overheating and cause the animal to become too fat, in which case it may well refuse to breed.

Hamsters also love peanuts, but they can cause overheating and obesity, if given in large amounts, they can also make the hamster smell if it has overindulged.

Biscuits and Other Foods

Biscuits usually consist of broken dog biscuits. They form a useful foodstuff, but are also helpful as the hamster has to gnaw them, and can therefore use them to wear down the teeth and therefore avoid overgrowing.

To supplement this basic diet, other foods can be added, for example bread, or small amounts of meat and eggs. Meat should only be given occasionally, and it should always be cooked and in very small amounts. Eggs should be hard boiled and cut into small pieces. Bread should be dried in the oven until very hard. Brown bread is preferable to white, as it contains wheatgerm.

Do not buy dry food for your hamster that is in any way discoloured, smells musty or damp. There is often a large amount of natural dust in certain seeds, however, which is quite normal.

Green Foods

Green foods should only be given in small amounts and, in fact, make very useful titbits. The list of plants that can be given is endless, but here are a few which are easily obtainable.

Any hamster owner with even a small kitchen garden, window box or allotment can probably grow a small amount of green foods to allow variety to be added to the diet at low cost all the year round.

Although lettuce is the most popular of all green foods for people to feed hamsters, it is dangerous in excess and can cause a serious liver complaint. Lettuce is a useful food, but in small amounts only.

Cabbage too can be dangerous if overfed to hamsters in any one meal. The outer leaves are the most beneficial, the inner having little food value in comparison, particularly in the white variety.

Cauliflower is without doubt the best of all cultivated vegetable greenstuffs. It has a less dramatic effect on the system than others, the leaves and stalks that are usually discarded by the cook are the best food value and can be cut up and fed to hamsters of all ages.

Chicory is another very good greenstuff, but it is rather difficult to obtain in certain areas of the country. It is not only good in food value but is also a valuable tonic.

Spinach is very strong tasting and some hamsters take a dislike to it for this reason, however, do try your stock on it as it is very rich in both vitamins and minerals.

Brussels sprouts and sprout tops are commonly fed to hamsters, but Brussels are not particularly suitable, as if fed in excess they can cause a wide variety of bladder complaints.

Kale is a much-overlooked vegetable that can be provided as green food. All the plant, apart from the roots, can be fed so there is no waste. In appearance it is much like cabbage, the most popular variety and the easiest to obtain is probably the curly kale.

The perennial herb, parsley will provide green food all year around, year after year. As with spinach, however, you may find that some stock will not like the taste.

The leaves and young shoots of the raspberry plant are a useful addition to the hamster's diet. It is especially useful if the animal is suffering from diarrhoea as its slight astringence dries up the system.

The safest of all root crops, carrots, can be obtained and fed to hamsters all the year round.

Clover is a very useful food item both as a green food or dried into hay.

Flowers

The flowers of your garden also produce an amazing variety of foods. You can feed quite a large variety of flowers but always avoid the flowers and leaves of the bulbs, as these are usually poisonous to livestock.

Among the more common flowers that can be fed are marigolds, nasturtium, phlox, rose, asters, michaelmas daisies, wallflowers, salvias, sweet peas, cornflowers and alyssum.

Although the common plants of the garden are easy to recognise, wild flowers and plants present quite a different picture as they are not always familiar – also many are very suitable, while others are highly dangerous. It is impossible to list all those plants that are suitable as there are so many, but this list gives those which are most common. If you do not know what the plants look like, do check with a plant identification guide and do not pick plants if you are not sure what they are.

Bramble	Knot grass
Blackberry	Mallow
Burnet	Nipplewort
Cow parsley	Plaintain
Coltsfoot	Shepherds purse
Crosswort	Sow thistle
Chickweed	Trefoil
Dandelion	Vetch
Dock	Watercress
Groundsel	Yarrow
Hedge parsley	

It is essential that you know what you are feeding to your hamster as a large number of plants are dangerous to stock. For example even the simple buttercup is lethal to a hamster. Also, never take a whole plant as this is illegal, and make sure that you are not collecting from any area sprayed with chemicals or visited by animals. Remember if in doubt leave it out!

Things To Remember When Feeding Your Hamster

There is a tendency for many hamster owners to give their pets very unsuitable foods simply because they are eating them themselves. For example, chocolate and other sweets should be avoided at all costs as the hamster's pouch is dry and it would be likely to get the sweet stuck to the delicate lining and be unable to remove it.

Remember that should you feed your hamster vegetable matter, it should only be in very small amounts at any one time.

Water

There has always been argument as to whether it is necessary to provide liquid for hamsters or not. I always advise that hamsters have water available 24 hours a day seven days a week. The best way to provide this is a gravity filled feeding bottle. These are available from most pet shops and can be obtained at the same time as you obtain your cage.

Hoarding

Your hamster will always want to hoard its food, although some hoard much more than others. A female with young is especially keen on storing food. An adult hamster will keep its hoard in one area of its cage and will usually try to keep it as far away from its toilet area as possible.

Do not change the litter or dispose of the hoarded food more than once a week, and when you do always return a little of the hoard to the place where you found it. This way, the hamster will know that the hoard is safe, and it will prevent your hamster from carrying around a part of its hoard in its pouches all the time, which may cause an infection.

7 Health

On the whole hamsters are very healthy little animals. The one question however that is asked again and again is what is the small brown patch on each hip of the male? Are they wounds? In fact, although these patches are more often noticed on males they do occur in both sexes, and they are scent glands. They are used in the wild to mark the walls of each individual animal's tunnel to show that it is already occupied.

Most hamsters are healthy and die of old age rather than any illness. However, bad management does account for a number of deaths. The majority of these are caused by feeding the wrong foods and using the wrong bedding.

This is not to say that hamsters never become ill. I will therefore mention a few of the more common ailments that may occur. Should your hamster appear ill and you are unsure what to do, please do not have a wild guess, take it to your local veterinary surgeon.

Wounds and Cuts

A hamster's flesh heals very quickly, and slight cuts and wounds are not in themselves dangerous. The most common cause of these wounds are sharp edges to the cage or the hamster's toys. Fights when mating or between litter mates are another cause, although if the hamsters are carefully watched these should not occur. Only very deep wounds or cuts need to be dealt with by the vet. Most cuts can be bathed in a mild antiseptic solution once a day.

Constipation

A blockage of the intestines caused by unsuitable bedding such as cotton wool, wood waste, kapok or newspaper is the most common reason for constipation. Naturally all bedding should be replaced with good meadow hay, and fresh green foods should be given in larger amounts than normal. Should constipation persist for more than 24 hours, then consult your vet.

Diarrhoea

This should not be confused with wet tail. It is the looseness of droppings, and is more often than not caused by the overfeeding of green vegetables.

Wet Tail

This is the most dangerous disease that a hamster can get. It is highly infectious and is invariably fatal. Little is known, however, as to its causes or treatment. In the first stages the hamster loses its normal sleek looks and becomes a rather sad creature with no appetite. The fur around the tail then becomes wet and a messy jelly-like fluid comes from the vent. Unfortunately death usually follows soon after.

Should wet tail be suspected the animal should be isolated away from any other hamsters and should be fed and dealt with only after you have dealt with the others. It is a highly infectious disease and can easily wipe out an entire stud of hamsters within a few weeks. Should the infected animal die, the cage and all items in it must be washed in very strong hot disinfectant before being used again. Also always wash your hands in strong disinfectant after handling an animal thought to have have this disease.

Should an animal recover from this disease it is unwise to try and breed from it as it is likely that the young may also suffer, although this is by no means certain.

Hibernation

Whether or not Golden hamsters hibernate in the wild has never been established, and it has been said that they do not, in the strict sense of the word, hibernate in captivity, but in fact become comatose.

Whichever is right, it is a fact that some hamsters subjected to a sudden drop in temperature, curl up and go into a deep sleep which can easily be mistaken for death. In this state the breathing becomes so shallow that it is hardly noticeable and only an occasional twitch of the whiskers shows that life is still present. Do not try to wake up the hamster by shaking it or poking it. Place the cage in a warm room, but not too near a fire – gradual heat is by far the best method to wake the hamster up.

It should not be too long before at least some signs of life are seen.

Do not assume that hamsters kept in an unheated outdoor shed will have this trouble while those indoors will not. Always give an ample supply of bedding to all hamsters in winter. Make sure, too, that the hamster is hibernating before you put him in a warm room, as some animals will inevitably die in winter.

8 **Breeding Hamsters**

Sexing Hamsters

In adult hamsters it is quite easy to distinguish between the sexes. The body shape of the female is more rounded at the rear and generally she is slightly larger than the male. The male is more elongated at the rear with a definite bulge near the base of the tail. It is in this bulge that the testes are concealed.

During mating or in certain weather conditions the testes of the male may be withdrawn into the body area and this may make the sexes more difficult to tell apart. However if you examine the underparts by turning the individuals over, the sex will again be quite clear. In the female the vaginal opening is quite close to the anus or vent, usually no more than 1-2 cm (½-¾ inch) away. The male will have a much wider gap between his anus and penile opening. A further indication of sex is the seven pairs of teats visible on the abdomen of the female.

Breeding

The breeding of hamsters should only be attempted by genuine enthusiasts who know the animals well and have cared for them for

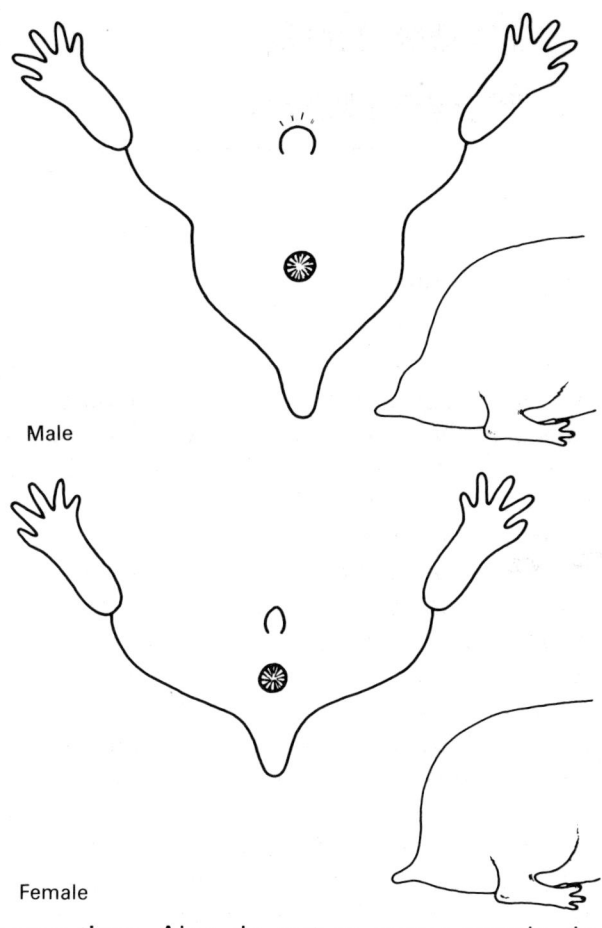

Male

Female

some time. Also do not as many people do, expect to make money out of breeding them. Should you decide that you wish to go into serious breeding of hamsters, contact an experienced breeder and ask him about the problems that it can entail. This is particularly important if you decide to breed one of the more difficult varieties. Breeders can often be contacted via your local pet shop or at local pet shows. Poor specimens are often the result of inexperienced breeding. In fact many poorly bred animals never really attain adult size, particularly when compared to top show animals, and lack condition and stamina, so do make sure you know what you are doing before you start.

Remember that hamsters have to be separated and placed in individual cages at quite an early age, so you must always ensure that you have either enough extra cages to contain a litter, or homes for them to go to straight away. Remember a litter may be as large as 16 hamsters.

Before being mated, male hamsters should be between 10 and 12 weeks and females at least 12 to 16 weeks. Breeding can take place throughout the year, although fewer litters are born in the winter months. Mating is best attempted in the late evening.

Females come onto heat every fourth or fifth day. It is not always possible to determine exactly when a female is on heat. Occasionally she may raise her tail when stroked lightly along her back, or she may be noticeably more active.

Mating must always be supervised as the female may very well attack the male if she is not in season. The male should never be taken to the female's cage as, even if she is on heat, she may attack him just because he has entered her cage. They have to be introduced on neutral ground, for example a spare cage, a bucket or a high-sided bowl. Place the male in the neutral area first, allowing him a time to have a sniff around and therefore get used to his surroundings, then introduce the female.

There is no reliable way of finding out whether a female is on heat, other than by trial and error. To find out, place her with the male on successive nights until she shows she is on heat by adopting the mating posture. The mating posture is very easy to recognise, the female will appear to freeze if put in with a male. As soon as the male pays her any close attention, she will stand quite still with ears erect, legs outstretched and tail held up stiffly. She will keep this position until the male has finished, stopping only for an occasional run around or perhaps a wash.

Until mating has commenced they should not be left alone or serious wounds may occur should they fight. If a fight should start, never attempt to break it up with your bare hands as you are then likely to be bitten by one or both animals. Instead use a piece of stiff card or wire mesh and place this between the animals. You can usually tell if a fight is about to start if you watch carefully; the best indication is that the male will roll over on to his back with the female on top, usually with a small mouthful of the male's flesh gripped in her teeth.

If the female is on heat the pair will mate for approximately 20 minutes. After this time they should be separated. On no account should they be left together overnight. The gestation period is 16 days and during this period the female should be handled as little as possible. She can have her litter in her normal cage, or you may prefer to use a special larger one, an old aquarium is ideal for this as it is warm, and the babies will be unable to squeeze through the bars of the cage when they start to crawl about. The cage should contain lots of sawdust and nesting material so that she can build herself a nest in plenty of time. Her food should naturally be increased slightly, particularly those foodstuffs that provide vitamins and proteins.

Although a litter has been known to number as many as 16 babies the average number is more likely to be six or seven. The babies are born naked and blind, and until they are approximately 36 hours old they are bright pink in colour. Their first fur appears at about five days and they then begin to develop rapidly, soon becoming active outside the nest. Their eyes open between 14 and 16 days at which time the diet of the mother, which has already been increased, should be increased still further.

It is a good idea while the litter are still in the nest to sprinkle wheat germ or Beemax powder around the edge as this will encourage the young to move about and supplement the diet they are receiving from the mother. Milk can also be given to the family, I always advise that this be given in a drinking bottle rather than a bowl, as I have seen young hamsters, crawling around before their eyes are open, fall into the bowls and drown.

The cage itself will probably become rather messy during the period of time that the litter are in the nest, but do not attempt to clean it out fully until the babies have their eyes open. Nor should the nest itself be disturbed before the litter are at least ten days old.

Weaning takes place at 21 to 24 days and the litter should be separated from the mother after about 26 days. Before the age of six weeks the entire litter should be separated into single sexed groups. They can remain together as long as they are playful and show no aggression towards one another. At the first signs of fighting, they must be placed into individual cages.

The mother should not be allowed to have another litter for at least four weeks. It is unlikely that a female will breed after the age of fourteen months, although a male may well breed for a few months longer.

Breeding Records

Should you decide to breed hamsters for either show or colour, the importance of keeping accurate and up to date breeding records cannot be emphasised too strongly. It is most important that a breeder can see at a glance which stock has been bred from which individuals, and which combination produces the best results.

By far the simplest way of doing this is to give each individual a hamster card. This card can either be fixed to the cage or stored in an index box. You should record such information as the name of the animal, its parents, grandparents, colour, age, the date of all litters borne or sired by it, the size of each litter, and the colours bred.

From information that is contained on these cards, detailed pedigrees can be formulated, and should a rare mutation be produced its ancestry can then be traced back and it maybe therefore possible to produce another by the same means.

Black Eyed Cream Long-haired female and litter of 14 day old young

9 **Dwarf Varieties of Hamster**

Unlike the Golden hamster the dwarf species do not really enjoy being kept on their own, and it has been suggested that to do so reduces their life span. They can be kept in pairs or groups of different or the same sex but the details of this will be given under how to look after each species.

The Chinese Hamster

The Chinese Hamster (*Cricetulus griseus*) has a varied history in captivity in Britain. At times being very popular and then falling from grace. What is certain is that it has been kept in laboratories off and on since at least 1919.

The original stocks were obtained from various wild captures in Mongolia, China and Manchuria, however it is thought that the stocks at present in Britain originated from animals captured just outside Peking in 1925.

In size it is one of the smallest of the hamsters being approximately 8-13 cm (3-5 ins) in length with quite a long tail. In colour it is brownish with a black dorsal stripe and a whitish-grey belly. Youngsters tend to be rather greyer than the adults.

Recently, a mutation of this species has occurred which is in the hands of very few breeders. It is a white-spotted variety, and although by no means certain, it is thought that this is a dominant gene. The ground colour is the normal brownish and this is broken in various amounts by patches of white over the entire dorsal area. The belly is much whiter than in the normal hamsters, and the patching varies greatly between individuals. Unfortunately little is known about when or where this mutation originally occurred.

Chinese Hamsters (normal colour variety)

Although Chinese Hamsters are easy to keep they are often rather quarrelsome among themselves. The females are particularly prone to nibbling and biting the male's tail and the genital region. I have found, however, that this occurs much less often when an exercise wheel is provided. It appears that this helps the female use up her aggressive energy.

This species appears to be able to survive cold much better than it can heat, and is known to have bred at 15°C (59°F) although the ideal temperature is 21°C (70°F). It is thought that this is also the reason for the large pronounced scrotal sack of the male. The Chinese hamsters are for this reason as easy to sex as the Golden hamster.

Caging of Chinese hamsters can be a problem as they tend to be able to squeeze through the bars of cages designed for Golden hamsters. I would therefore suggest that they be kept either in the laboratory cages that can be obtained from specialist suppliers or in a converted aquarium. The latter is particularly useful if you decide to keep a colony rather than a pair.

I have found that a suitable colony may be established with a minimum of two males and three females. These should be kept in a tank of about 60 cm (24 ins) long with 5 cm (2 ins) litter base. Also included in the tank should be some plastic or earthenware pipes and a few twigs on which to climb. The pipes will serve as nest boxes and also allow the animals to avoid each other if they want to. In my own colony I have also included a wheel.

Smaller units can be used for pairs or single sexed groups, but with a colony you are likely to have much more activity. If you are breeding for colour, however, it is more advisable to retain them in pairs.

The gestation period after mating is 20 days to 21 days, although 16 days have been recorded. Although large litters are born, there is a tendency for Chinese females to cull the litter to four or six. At birth they are naked and blind but they do have teeth and whiskers. The skin darkens at about three days, and even at this stage the dorsal stripe is visible. The fur appears at six to eight days and the eyes open at fourteen days. Solid food will be taken from nine days. They are independent at 18 to 21 days and are able to breed at 90 days. The average lifespan is 18 to 24 months.

Their food requirements are basically the same as the Golden hamster but with the addition of a larger amount of vegetable matter. Water should always be available as lack of it appears to cause fighting.

White Chinese Hamsters

Dwarf Russian Hamsters

Also known as the Djungarian, Striped, and Hairy Footed Hamster, the Dwarf Hamster (*Phodopus sungoris*), as it is more commonly known, is only about 8 cm (3 ins) in length with a very short tail that is usually hidden by the thick fur. The female is usually slightly smaller than the male.

The most commonly seen of the two sub-species at present available in Britain is the western variety. The coat colour is brownish grey with a conspicuous yet fine black dorsal stripe; the belly fur is a buffish white. In this sub-species there is at present one mutation, which again is only in the hands of a few breeders, including myself. It is not, however, a coat colour mutation but it is a coat type, the Satin, and in this species it is a recessive gene. This mutation was discovered in the south of England by Peter Marsh and the records of its breeding are being carefully retained.

The less common eastern sub-species is darker, being more grey than brown, and slightly larger with a short muzzle and larger, more rounded ears. It also has the unusual characteristic of turning white in the short days of winter; sixteen hours dark, eight hours light. Both sub-species have well developed cheek pouches, but they are used less frequently than in their larger cousins. The two sub-species are known by the names Original and White.

The Dwarf Russian Hamster was first kept in this country in 1963 by the Zoological Society of London but it was not reported as breed-

Russian Hamsters, 3 week old babies

Russian Hamsters, winter white variety

ing until 1968. It has also been retained by a number of laboratories. The Original was introduced onto the pet market from stock obtained by Mr Percy Parslow from the ZSL in the early 1970s. The Whites were later to arrive, having being introduced to the pet market by myself in 1978 from stock obtained from the former colony at Queen Mary College, London.

The Russian is as easy to keep in captivity as the Chinese, presenting the same caging problems. I have found that although they will live very happily in colonies they are much happier in pairs either of opposite or the same sex.

A pair that has a litter left with them will often refuse to breed again until the litter is removed. However, I have known pairs that have produced a litter before the previous litter is even properly weaned. The males make wonderful fathers, if given half the chance by the female, helping with the nest building and keeping the young warm while the female is feeding, although as with all aspects of life it does depend on the individual. The gestation period is usually about 20 to 21 days, although 16 has been recorded. The litter size is smaller than the Chinese, averaging only four. The development of the young is much the same as the Chinese, and although they can be sexed in the same way as both the Golden and Chinese, it is much less easy to do so at a glance. The diet is also similar, and again water should always be available.

Lastly, if one of a pair should die, be prepared for the fact that you may not be able to introduce another animal to it, whatever the sex.

10 Clubs and Societies

Throughout the world there are a number of clubs, societies and circles that promote the breeding and showing of hamsters. Since these clubs do not maintain separate office premises, but operate from the homes of the officers of the day it is impossible to quote addresses. Your local breeder should be able to give you information on clubs in your area.